MW00617924

To my handsome husband Greg:
Thank you for saying,

"Honey, don't worry, everything's DAPO."

CREDITS

Inspired by: God
Authored by: Susan Day
Encouraged by: Greg Grabacki
Edited by: Cat Knarr
Cover and interior designed by: Gaige Larson
DAPO logo designed by: Holly Dickens, Ellen Senrich
Susan's photo taken by: Sarah Marentette
Marketed and Managed by: Raising The Standard, LLC, Steve Hoeft

ISBN: 978-0-9909888-0-9
DAPO Publishing
Chicago, Illinois
www.DAPO.me
sday@dapo.me

The following book includes several translations of the Holy Bible.

BEFORE YOU BEGIN...

What started as a simple desire to inspire people has become a movement. And just by picking up this book, you've become part of it—there's no turning back now!

Six years ago, I started posting daily inspirational messages and personal challenges on social media. I wanted to encourage people to wake up, to live in the light, and to realize that God has a perfect plan for their lives—even in the midst of uncertainty, chaos, and pain.

What happened next surprised me. A virtual community formed around the world. Readers left their comments and feedback. And, many contacted me to encourage me to keep writing these words of wisdom. As I read their comments, I was struck how similar we all are—regardless of age, ethnicity, gender, religion, or income. We all get stuck from time to time, and we feel like we can't move forward. I also recognized we share three basic needs: we want to be seen, we yearn to be heard, and we ache to know that someone relates to our pain. It was remarkable how many times readers reached out to ask if I was in their homes spying on their families and writing directly to them. Of course, I laughed and responded, "I can only write these posts because I've *lived* them."

I'm often asked, "Were you always this way—full of faith, hope, and light?" The short answer is, "No."

I *became* Susan Day through years of living in darkness. I know firsthand the pain, heartache, and struggles that accompany an abusive relationship, an eating disorder, substance abuse, and workaholism. I also know the disappointment of divorce and the unrequited desire to have a child. As a young woman I told my therapist, "Well, I guess the only addiction I don't have is gambling." After a fleeting pause, I cried out, "Put me down for gambling too. After all, I've been playing Russian roulette with my life!" That was twenty-four years ago.

Today, I'm beyond grateful to be standing strongly in the light of day. No, the journey wasn't easy. It was like a poorly choreographed dance with steps forward, backward, and sideways. It was long, and at times, excruciatingly painful. And yet, I don't have regrets. Yes, there are choices I wish I'd made differently. And I wouldn't be the woman I am today without those experiences.

I liken my journey to the formation of a pearl. It's truly miraculous. A natural pearl begins its life as an irritating grain of sand, which has been lodged in an oyster's soft inner body. To ease this irritant, the oyster's body produces nacre—a soft, soothing substance that becomes strong, resilient, and iridescent. As long as the irritant remains within its body, the oyster will continue to coat it with layer upon layer of nacre.

Like the grain of sand, *I* was the irritant in my own life. The choices I made held me captive inside a hard dark place. But our miraculous God met me there, and began to coat me with the nacre of life lessons that He had prepared for me. Like the nacre, layer upon layer, He used these lessons to transform me until it was time for me to emerge—strong, resilient, and ready to reflect His light. Now I'm called to share what I've learned with you.

I have collected 52 of these life lessons and offer them to you in this companion journal, called ***Divine And Perfect Order:*** *52 Simple Truths, Simple Tools & Simple Words of Wisdom for Your Life*. True to the book's title, each journal entry includes:

SIMPLE WORDS OF WISDOM: my advice for tackling the tough issues in your life. Mark the entries that resonate with you the most so you can return to them when you need encouragement.

A SIMPLE TRUTH: a Bible verse to inspire and motivate you. Read it and move on, or go deeper by looking up the context, memorizing the verse, or praying over that passage.

A SIMPLE TOOL: a thought-provoking question, personal challenge, or practical action step. Use this page as your free writing space to journal your thoughts, goals, and prayers.

This book is *your* companion. It's an invitation to look within, clearly see how you're spending your life, and write your heart out. My hope and heartfelt prayer is that this journal helps you get closer to God and the life you desire. You have the power to choose how you want to live. You have the choice to pursue the life you say you want—and more importantly, the life God has called you to. Use these life lessons to take your next step forward.

There is no right or wrong way to read this book. Simply open it and trust God to lead you to the right entries. Read them all at once, or savor them one at a time. Read one a day for 52 days, or read one a week for a year. Journal as you go along. And ask God where you need to grow and change.

You can keep this journal to yourself if you like. After all, it's a place for your most personal thoughts and most intimate prayers. And, if you find yourself yearning to reach out to someone else, to share what you're learning or what you're going through, then don't hold back. Find a friend to talk to. Reach out to me at sday@dapo.me. And talk to other readers who are working their way through this journal—I created a private Facebook group just for that, visible only to its members. Join that community at **www.facebook.com/groups/DivineAndPerfectOrder.**

When I talk about God's Divine And Perfect Order, I call it **DAPO**. That's my husband's creation. One day in the midst of a difficult situation, my husband Greg confidently turned to me and said, "Honey, don't worry, everything's DAPO." Since I hadn't had my morning cup of coffee yet, I gave him a puzzled look and asked what he meant. Greg said, "Well, *you* always say, 'Everything's in God's divine and perfect order.' So trust, everything's DAPO!"

Indeed, everything is **DAPO**. It's in **God's Divine And Perfect Order**. And you're *never* alone on this journey. If you risk opening your shell just a little bit, God will guide you deeper into His loving light. I will be praying for you each step of the way.

"Everything's DAPO!"

WORDS OF WISDOM

"EVERYTHING'S DAPO!"

It's in God's Divine And Perfect Order.

Trust God in your current circumstance, despite your present understanding, and He'll direct you. Even in the midst of pain, chaos, and uncertainty, He is in control. Everything is in God's Divine And Perfect Order—or as I like to call it, DAPO®. You might be lost in a cloud of uncertainty, but the clarity and peace you've been longing for isn't far away, perhaps behind a door you didn't think to open. When everything comes together in an 'only God' kind of way, that's a DAPO moment. It reflects God's Divine And Perfect Order. Trust God. He has the answer to the question you have been asking. DAPO is more than an acronym. It's a way of living, a deep knowledge that God is in control. When fear and doubt threaten your sense of security, repeat this truth out loud: "Everything's DAPO!"

SIMPLE TRUTH

"For God is not a God of disorder but of peace."
1 Corinthians 14:33 (NIV)

SIMPLE TOOL

Trust "Everything's DAPO!"

The world is filled with ordinary and astonishing moments of synchronicity that defy an easy explanation. Pay attention to how God is working in your life. Start by making a list of five DAPO moments you've experienced so far:

1

2

3

4

5

WORDS OF WISDOM

THERE'S WISDOM IN WAITING.

Do you find it difficult to wait? Are you impatient? Wait isn't a dirty, four-letter word. It's an opportunity to **W**illingly ***A***nticipate the ***I***deal ***T***ime. Making wise decisions often requires time—time to pray, discuss, and weigh your options. Ask these three questions prior to making every important decision:

1. What will happen if I don't make a decision?
2. What will happen if I wait a day or two?
3. What will happen if I do make a decision?

The answers to these questions may help you determine how quickly you need to make a decision and the potential ramifications. When anyone presses you to make a quick decision, that's often a warning to WAIT. Take extra time before giving your answer. Few things are so critical that you must answer immediately. The next time you have to make a significant decision, remember it's wise to wait.

SIMPLE TRUTH

"Wait for the LORD; be strong and take heart and wait for the LORD."
Psalm 27:14 (NIV)

SIMPLE TOOL

Learn to wait.

What significant decision are you facing today? Answer these questions before you decide:

1. What additional information do I need to get?

   ____

2. Who can serve as a sounding board and offer me wise advice?

   ____

   Take this person out for coffee and talk it out.

3. What will happen if I make a decision? If I don't? Should I wait?

   ____

   ____

4. List the pros and cons:

PROS	CONS
______________	______________
______________	______________
______________	______________
______________	______________
______________	______________

WORDS OF WISDOM

YOUR WORDS ARE POWERFUL.

Words have real power. They do more than just convey information. They have the power to leave a lasting impression. Words build up, and words bulldoze. Words encourage, and words destroy. Words lighten the spirit, and words darken the soul. Words survive the test of time. Words spoken decades ago can be recalled in an instant, or they can reverberate for a lifetime. When you know the power of your words, you'll be careful in your conversations. You only have to watch the reaction on someone's face to know the power and impact of your words.

SIMPLE TRUTH

"The tongue has the power of life and death."
Proverbs 18:21 (NIV)

SIMPLE TOOL

Watch your words.

Replay the last few conversations you had today. What did you say? How will you change your words to be more uplifting and positive?

DAY 3

WORDS OF WISDOM

YOUR THOUGHTS DETERMINE YOUR BEHAVIOR.

If you feed it, it will grow. It's just that simple. When you water a plant, it grows. When you exercise your mind, it grows. And, if you feed your anger, dysfunction, and disappointment, they grow too! Every time you feed your negative thoughts—the hurt, regret, and shame—they grow. It's up to you to stop rehashing the depressing details, reliving the negative memory, and retelling that agonizing story. Yes, it was painful, wrong, and perhaps even illegal or immoral. And, it's over. Dwelling on your pain won't change anything. Decide today to stop feeding your destructive thoughts.

SIMPLE TRUTH

"Fix your thoughts on what is true, and honorable, and right, and pure, and lovely, and admirable. Think about things that are excellent and worthy of praise."
Philippians 4:8 (NLT)

SIMPLE TOOL

Nourish your mind.

The most important messages you hear are the ones you tell yourself. Program your thoughts to be positive. Start by spending a moment in silence. Ask the Holy Spirit to show you where you need to think more positively. Complete the following statements:

"I can ______________________________
____
______________________________."

"I will ______________________________
____
______________________________."

"I am ______________________________
____
______________________________."

DAY 4

TAKE RESPONSIBILITY FOR YOUR CHOICES.

It's never too late, if you want tomorrow to be different than today. However, you must be willing to take responsibility for ALL of your choices. Everything you do is based on the choices you make. Don't make excuses. Refuse to point your finger at your childhood, the economy, an employer, a previous relationship, your spouse, or even your age. Take responsibility for your choices today and you'll change the course of your future tomorrow. People will respect you more when you own your choices. It's not too late!

SIMPLE TRUTH

"For we must all stand before Christ to be judged."
2 Corinthians 5:10a (NLT)

SIMPLE TOOL

Take responsibility.

Identify three areas where you want to change. Next to each item, list one small step you will take today.
It's never too late.

	Where I Want to Change	Step I Will Take
1	______	______
2	______	______
3	______	______

WORDS OF WISDOM

HONOR YOUR WORD.

Life is easier when you know people's expectations and when you communicate yours. Be honest and straightforward. Make commitments only after you've considered what it will take to keep them. Consider this: When speaking with others, ask them to tell you upfront what you can expect from them. Express your preference to know the complete picture and to be made aware of all changes and delays immediately. The same is true when you make a commitment to someone. Be honest. If something changes, communicate it. When you do, there's no room for confusion.

SIMPLE TRUTH

"Just say a simple, 'Yes, I will,' or 'No, I won't.'"
Matthew 5:37 (NLT)

SIMPLE TOOL

Manage people's expectations.

Who do you have a conflict or misunderstanding with? Have you been completely open with that person? Practice writing what you will say to them.

DAPO 6

WORDS OF WISDOM

PAIN HAS A PURPOSE.

Pain, whether it comes in the form of relational conflict, individual struggle, or spiritual trial, is part of life. Regardless of how pain makes its way in, it offers valuable lessons and the potential for tremendous personal and spiritual growth. How you choose to cope with pain determines how you'll process it and what you'll learn. Stop treating pain like an unwanted house guest, wishing it would leave as soon as it arrives. Rather, embrace it. Learn the lessons it came to teach. And, know your pain is never wasted. Even Jesus wept.

SIMPLE TRUTH

"Here on earth you will have many trials and sorrows. But take heart, because I have overcome the world."
John 16:33 (NLT)

SIMPLE TOOL

Learn from pain.

Painful patterns tend to repeat until you truly get the lesson. How do you typically respond to pain? Write it out.

Do you see a pattern? Understanding that pattern will help you respond differently next time.

DAPO 7

WORDS OF WISDOM

YOU ARE RESPONSIBLE *TO* OTHERS AND *FOR* YOURSELF.

You wouldn't build a house without knowing where the property lines begin and end. Likewise, you have to know and communicate your boundaries when building a relationship. Drawing the lines clearly demonstrates what you will and will not tolerate. Healthy relationships build their foundation on the clear understanding of each person's boundaries and their respective roles. Typically there's a price to pay for disrespecting someone's property. The same should be true for your boundaries. (For example, if your spouse speaks to you in a disrespectful tone, you can stop the conversation and state you are happy to resume the discussion after your spouse walks away and calms down.) It's your responsibility to clearly spell out the consequences for crossing your boundaries. Boundaries without clearly stated consequences are ineffective.

SIMPLE TRUTH

"For we are each responsible for our own conduct."
Galatians 6:5 (NLT)

SIMPLE TOOL

Know and communicate your boundaries.

Identify your boundaries. Complete these three sentences with at least five examples.

People may not ______________________.
______________________.
______________________.
______________________.
______________________.

Examples: Go through my personal possessions; criticize me publicly; offer their opinion about my weight; take their anger out on me; humiliate me in front of others; tell racist jokes in my company; invade my personal space.

I have a right to ask for ______________________.
______________________.
______________________.
______________________.
______________________.

Examples: Privacy; more information before making a commitment; quiet time alone; help around the house; silence while getting a facial; my hair to be cut the way I want; someone to remove their shoes in my home.

To protect my time and energy, it's okay to
______________________.
______________________.
______________________.
______________________.
______________________.

Examples: Not answer the phone when it rings; cancel a commitment if I'm sick; choose not to text; reserve a quiet corner in my home that's all mine; ask people not to call after 9 p.m.

WORDS OF WISDOM

GOD HEARS AND DELIVERS.

If you want to remember how close and personal God is, keep a Deliverance Diary. It's simple. When you have a prayer request or question, jot it down. Then when God gives you direction, record and date it. Trials, painful times, and seasons of waiting are certain. And when you commit to keeping a Deliverance Diary, you'll always have a personal record of how and when God showed up and delivered you. Keep this diary, and you'll never have to wonder again if God hears you or still answers your prayers. The proof is in your hands—it's in your Deliverance Diary.

SIMPLE TRUTH

"The righteous cry out, and the Lord hears them;
he delivers them from all their troubles."
Psalm 34:17 (NIV)

SIMPLE TOOL

Keep a Deliverance Diary to remind you of God's presence.

You have celebrated God's intervention in your life many times and many ways. Write down five ways God has answered and delivered you in the past. Start recording these times regularly.

1

2

3

4

5

DAY 9

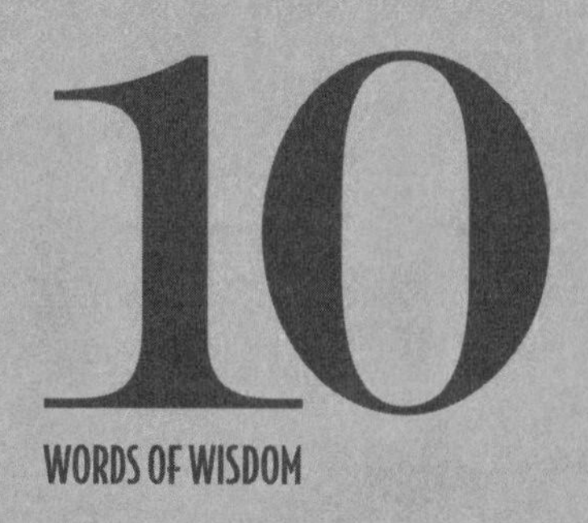

YOU ARE VALUABLE.

The amount of money you make doesn't determine your value or worth. Your significance is not measured by your profession, your title, or what's written in Box #1 on your W-2. Money is something you make. It doesn't make you who you are.

SIMPLE TRUTH

"I praise you because I am fearfully and wonderfully made; your works are wonderful, I know that full well."
Psalm 139:14 (NIV)

SIMPLE TOOL

Appreciate how you were created.

You are unique, one of a kind. Notice your eyes blinking. Feel your lungs as they fill with air. Study the pattern of your heartbeat. Wiggle your toes. Give thanks as you write five things that you appreciate about your body. Do this daily.

1

2

3

4

5

WORDS OF WISDOM

GRATITUDE ELEVATES YOUR ATTITUDE.

When you understand that gratitude is a choice, you change the lens through which you see the world. You'll notice and make time to celebrate your friendships. You might throw a luncheon for your special circle of friends, sharing memories that show how their friendship blesses you. You'll wake up thanking God for the gift and privilege of a new day. Commit to sharing your appreciation for your life by doing a random act of kindness for a complete stranger. Appreciation and gratitude walk hand in hand. Grab them with both hands.

SIMPLE TRUTH

"Sing and make music from your heart to the Lord, always giving thanks to God the Father for everything."
Ephesians 5:19-20 (NIV)

SIMPLE TOOL

Choose to be grateful.

Consider all the ways you have an abundant life. If you don't know where to start, make a list of those things you often take for granted, such as: your home, your ability to see or hear, healthy children, running water, and food. List ten items daily.

Start here.

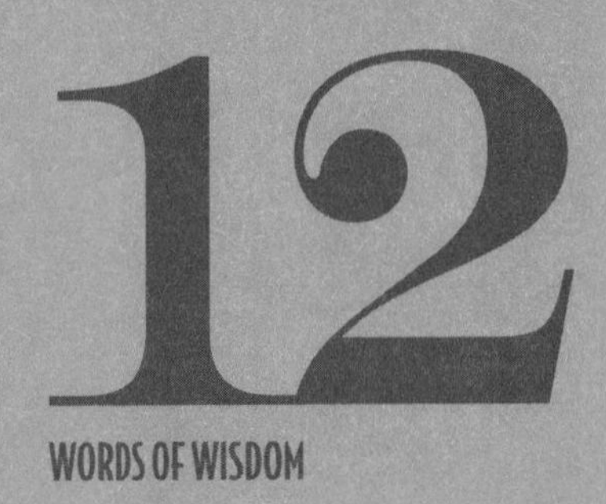

WORDS OF WISDOM

BE FLEXIBLE.

Life will stretch you in all sorts of directions. However, when you learn to be like Gumby, flexible and willing to bend, you don't have to break. Be willing to stretch to where God calls you.

SIMPLE TRUTH

"We can make our plans, but the LORD determines our steps."
Proverbs 16:9 (NLT)

SIMPLE TOOL

Be like Gumby.

Identify three areas where you tend to be inflexible and rigid. How do you respond in those situations?

Write it out:

1

2

3

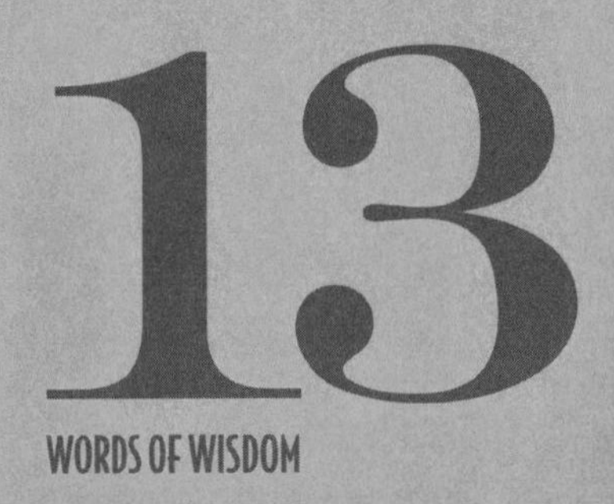

WORDS OF WISDOM

IF IT DOESN'T CONCERN YOU, STAY OUT OF IT.

Stop wasting time dwelling on things that are simply none of your business. Put them into your None-of-My-Business Bucket. What should you put in there? Anything that doesn't directly concern you. If you spend time digging for details, meddling, or gossiping, you're wasting time and energy. It's none of your business! Instead, write those nitpicking, energy-wasting, anxiety-producing things on slips of paper and throw them in your None-of-My-Business Bucket. Stop and ask yourself, "Is this any of my business?" If not, you know where to put it.

SIMPLE TRUTH

"Make it your goal to live a quiet life, minding your own business and working with your hands, just as we instructed you before."
1 Thessalonians 4:11 (NLT)

SIMPLE TOOL

Get a None-of-My-Business Bucket.

Bad habits develop quickly. Notice when you gossip, when you focus on issues that don't concern you, and when you're tempted to take control. Name three things you can throw in your bucket right now.

1

2

3

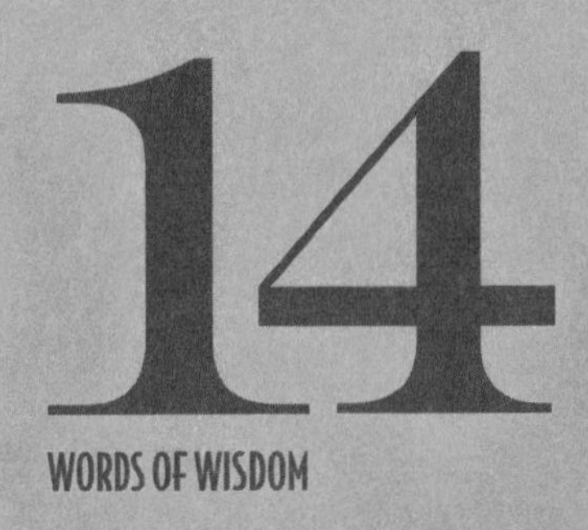

WORDS OF WISDOM

KNOW WHEN TO LET GO.

Knowing when to let go is essential for healthy living. Do you know how to let go of someone or something that's not good for you? Be willing to release that person or circumstance. When you surrender whatever holds you captive, you make room for God to take control. Try this: Make a tightly clenched fist. Now, close it even tighter. What can get in? *Answer:* Absolutely nothing. Now, unclench your fist and release and stretch out each finger. Now what can get in? That's right—everything! When you clench your fists around your life, that's a sign of a prideful spirit. Let go and surrender to God's timing and plan.

SIMPLE TRUTH

"A time to keep and a time to throw away."
Ecclesiastes 3:6 (NLT)

SIMPLE TOOL

Let go and trust God.

When fear grips you, you might try to hold on even tighter. What do you fear losing control of? Name it specifically. Journal your thoughts:

DAY 14

WORDS OF WISDOM

YOU CHOOSE WHEN AND WHERE TO PLUG IN.

If you find yourself asking, "When will the madness stop?" then here's a hint: It will stop when you stop participating in unhealthy relationships, habits, and thoughts. The best way to stop the madness is to kill the power. If there's an unhealthy person or habit damaging your life, you need to unplug. It's that simple. When you disconnect from that person, situation, or way of thinking, you preserve your energy. Don't plug in and the madness will stop.

SIMPLE TRUTH

"Come near to God and he will come near to you."
James 4:8 (NIV)

SIMPLE TOOL

Stop the madness.

List any unhealthy relationships, harmful habits, or negative thoughts you're participating in. How will you unplug? Identify one concrete step you will take today.

Unhealthy Relationships, Habits, and Thoughts:

Concrete Step I Will Take:

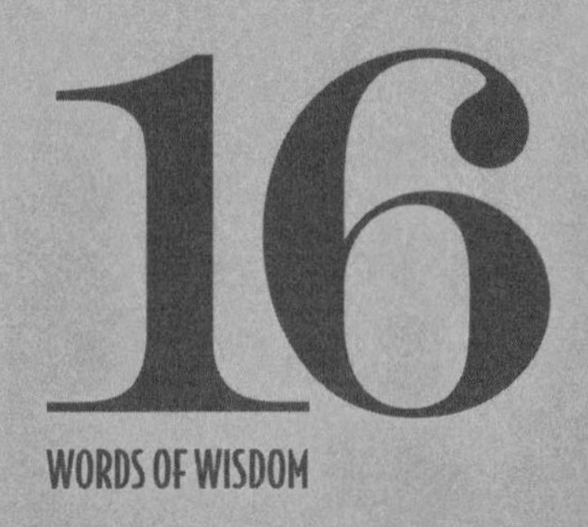

WORDS OF WISDOM

LOVE IS THE MOST BEAUTIFUL HOME ACCESSORY.

It doesn't matter where you live when your home is filled with the people you love. The size of your house, the location, or the view never makes a house a home. The loving people in your house make it a home. Your home will be filled with priceless treasures when you decorate it with love, joy, and peace.

SIMPLE TRUTH

"By wisdom a house is built, and through understanding it is established; through knowledge its rooms are filled with rare and beautiful treasures."
Proverbs 24:3-4 (NIV)

SIMPLE TOOL

Decorate your home with love.

How will you cultivate more love in your home today? Consider turning off cell phones at mealtime. Share one positive thought or memory with each family member daily. Tuck a love note in your spouse's work bag or child's lunch. Journal your creative ideas, and then do one today.

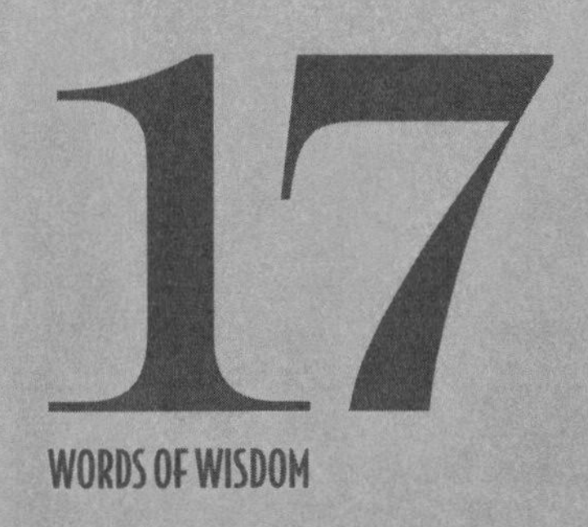

PEOPLE DON'T WANT TO HEAR YOUR NEGATIVITY.

Keep the duct tape handy for those days when you don't have anything encouraging, loving, or positive to say. Before you speak, ask yourself, "Are these words uplifting or necessary?" If not, imagine removing a small piece of duct tape and placing it over your mouth. Keep a roll in sight, on your dashboard, desk, or kitchen counter to serve as a reminder to guard your words. You alone are responsible for what passes over your lips and comes out of your mouth.

SIMPLE TRUTH

"Set a guard over my mouth, Lord;
keep watch over the door of my lips."
Psalm 141:3 (NIV)

SIMPLE TOOL

Keep the duct tape handy.

Own the power of your words. Try this experiment: For one week, commit to only speaking when you have something favorable or enriching to say. Record your observations daily. Start by journaling one positive thing you will say to someone important in your life.

What did you find?

18

WORDS OF WISDOM

DENIAL IS DESTRUCTIVE.

If you won't be honest with yourself, you can't be honest with anyone. If you deny, deflect, or downplay your role and responsibility, nothing will change. Your denial is destructive. It holds you and keeps you stuck, unable to move forward. Take an honest look at yourself—your motives, your thoughts, your actions, and everything that makes you who you are.

SIMPLE TRUTH

"Why do you look at the speck of sawdust in your brother's eye and pay no attention to the plank in your own eye?"
Matthew 7:3 (NIV)

SIMPLE TOOL

Look at yourself first.

Where are you denying responsibility? Are you ignoring your role in a broken relationship, an unrealized dream, or an addiction you're not willing to own? Ask a trusted friend to share what they've observed.

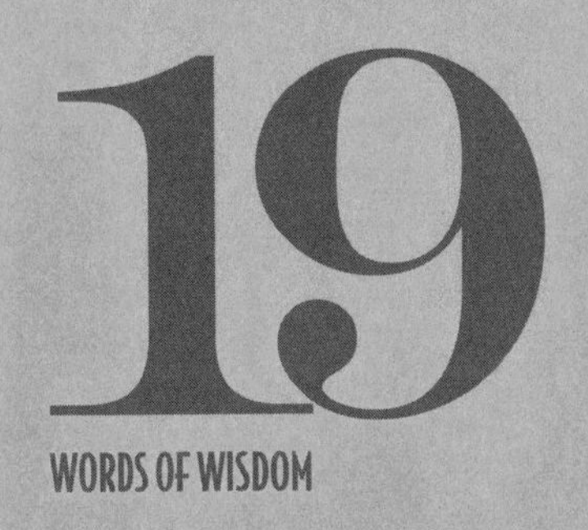

WORDS OF WISDOM

THERE'S NO REMEDY LIKE TIME ALONE WITH GOD.

Life can be hectic, stressful, and exhausting at times. No spa treatment can offer what God alone provides. If you need energy, rejuvenation, and renewal, spend time alone with Him. Find a quiet spot, be still, and simply ask God to replenish and refresh you. If you're too busy to spend time alone with God, change something. It's just that simple.

SIMPLE TRUTH

"Come to me, all you who are weary and burdened, and I will give you rest."
Matthew 11:28 (NIV)

SIMPLE TOOL

Spend quiet time with God to soothe your weary spirit.

Have you ever thought about your quiet time as an intimate conversation with God? What would you say to Him right now?

What distractions do you need to eliminate to develop a quiet time practice?

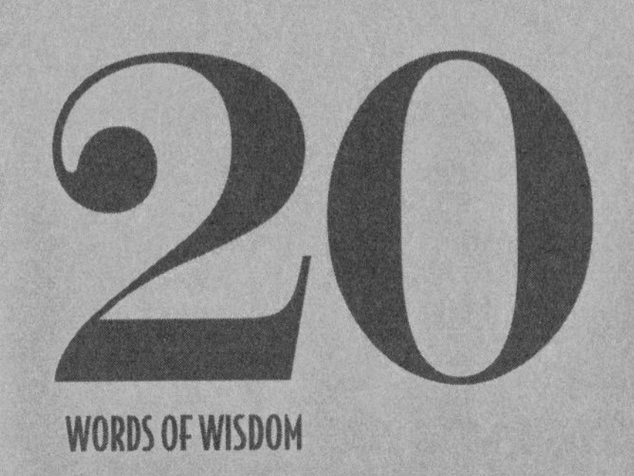

WORDS OF WISDOM

YOU HAVE TO DO SOMETHING TO CHANGE SOMETHING.

If the only things that have changed are the pages of the calendar or the hands on the clock, then nothing's really changed. Only time has passed. If you want your life to change, you must be willing to take new action. As the saying goes, "The definition of insanity is doing the same thing over and over again and expecting different results." What do you need to do that you haven't yet?

SIMPLE TRUTH

"Jesus told him, 'Stand up, pick up your mat, and walk!'"
John 5:8 (NLT)

SIMPLE TOOL

Take action.

Answer these questions:

Based on my daily activities and routines, where can I expect to be six months or a year from now?

Are the people I choose to associate with helping me or hurting me?

What excuses am I making?

What mistakes do I fear making most?

How have past rejections eroded my confidence?

What do I need to do next?

21

WORDS OF WISDOM

LISTEN TO YOUR BODY.

Your body has a built-in alarm system to alert you when something is wrong. Pay attention to your twitching eye, your racing heart, your nauseous stomach, or your fatigued body. They are the sirens and flashing lights cautioning you to pull over and reconsider your course. Stop and take this simple test: Ask yourself, "Am I deliberately disobeying God? Or, am I knowingly deceiving or dishonoring another or myself?" Don't dismiss the *dis*-ease in your body—it's warning you to make the necessary adjustments.

SIMPLE TRUTH

"Before I was afflicted I went astray, but now I obey your word."
Psalm 119:67 (NIV)

SIMPLE TOOL

Disobedience and deception bring *dis*-ease.

What happens in your body when something is not right? If you don't know, commit to being acutely aware the next time your body feels off-kilter. Name specifically where the pain or discomfort is located.

What will you do the next time you feel those warning signals?

22

WORDS OF WISDOM

A *TRUTH* FRIEND IS HARD TO FIND.

Find a wise person who is willing to tell you the truth, and you've found a good person to call your friend. Anyone can tell you what you want to hear. But true friends have your best interests in mind. They'll risk feeling uncomfortable to protect you. They'll share what others are unwilling or unable to see. They'll speak the truth. And, they'll hold up the mirror, as long as it takes, so you can see the truth for yourself. That's a true friend.

SIMPLE TRUTH

"As iron sharpens iron, so a friend sharpens a friend."
Proverbs 27:17 (NLT)

SIMPLE TOOL

Find a *truth* friend.

Who is your *truth* friend?

____

Write down three specific questions you will give your *truth* friend to hold you accountable.

Perhaps these questions are related to how you spent your time this week, healthy activities you need to make time for, or unhealthy activities you need to stop. You know where you need accountability.

1 ____

2 ____

3 ____

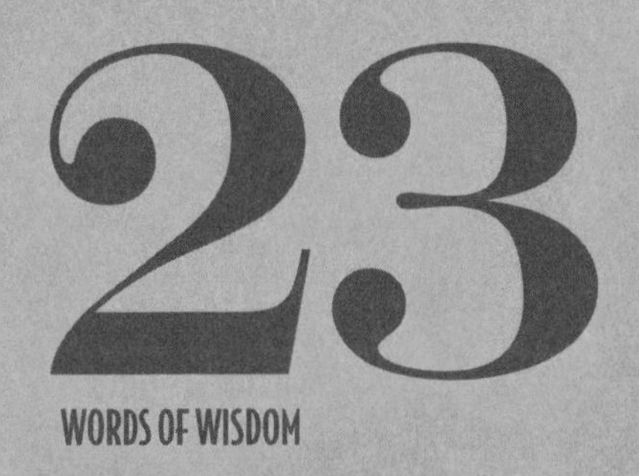

WORDS OF WISDOM

FAILING DOESN'T MAKE YOU A FAILURE.

If you want to grow, you must be willing to risk failing. When you do fail, that doesn't mean that you lost or have to give up. Rather, true failure only happens when you fail to take another risk for fear of failing again. Apply what you've learned to the next opportunity. Sometimes God orchestrates failure before He brings about success. Your failures can be steppingstones to growth—if you will learn from your mistakes.

SIMPLE TRUTH

"No discipline seems pleasant at the time, but painful. Later on, however, it produces a harvest of righteousness and peace for those who have been trained by it."
Hebrews 12:11 (NIV)

SIMPLE TOOL

Learn from failure.

When have you perceived yourself as a failure? What did you learn from those experiences?

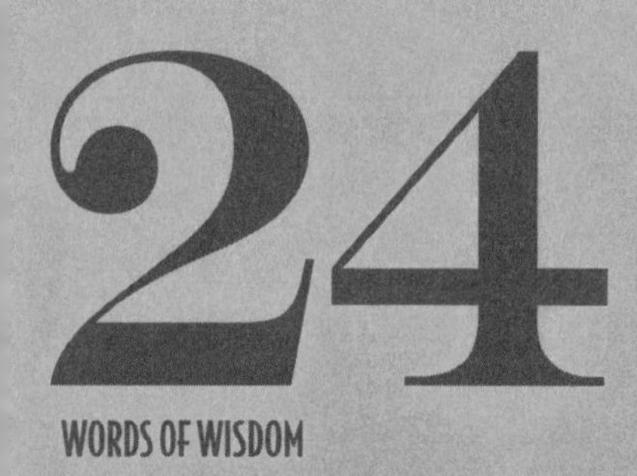

WORDS OF WISDOM

YOU WON'T ALWAYS BE PREPARED.

Sometimes life can feel like a game of "Duck, Duck, Goose." When you're tagged, you just have to get up and move quickly! And remember, there won't always be time to prepare. Just be willing to move when you get *goosed*. Duck, Duck, Duck...

SIMPLE TRUTH

"'Come, follow me,' Jesus said. ... At once they left their nets and followed him."
Matthew 4:19-20 (NIV)

SIMPLE TOOL

Realize you won't always have your ducks in a row.

Yes, it's uncomfortable to get up and move when you're not prepared. Recall a recent experience when you felt unprepared. Describe the situation. What was the result? Accept that you won't always be ready when you're asked to move.

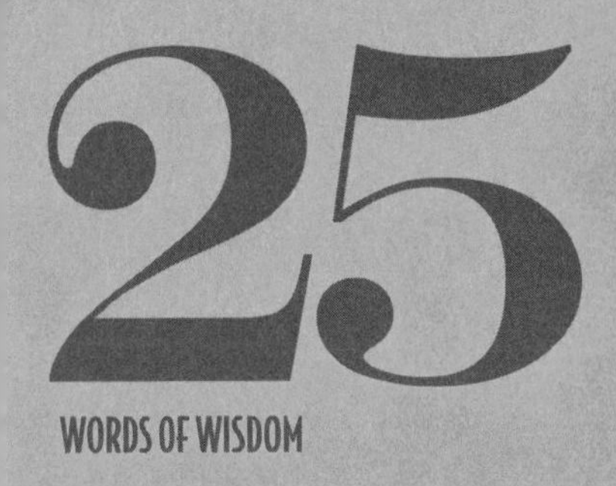

CHILDREN ARE DIRECT. LEARN FROM THEM.

Spend a few minutes with a child and here's what you'll quickly learn: Children live in the moment. If they want something, they ask for it. When they've lost interest in what you're saying, you'll know. And, you never have to wonder what they're thinking; they'll tell you. Now, those are a few great lessons we can all learn. Live like a child. Be present. Be honest. Be direct.

SIMPLE TRUTH

"And he said: 'Truly I tell you, unless you change and become like little children, you will never enter the kingdom of heaven.'"
Matthew 18:3 (NIV)

SIMPLE TOOL

Learn from children.

Spend time with a child. If you don't have children, offer to care for a friend's child for an hour or two.

Watch. Listen. Learn. What did you observe? What did you hear that piqued your curiosity? How can you apply what you've learned from children in your life?

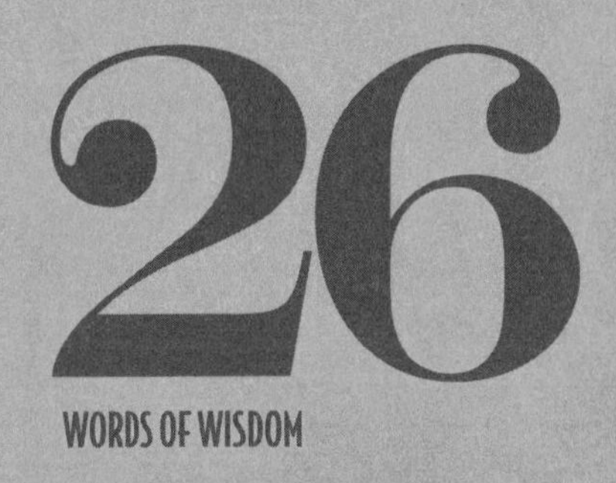

IT'S NOT ALL ABOUT YOU.

So much of what happens in life is simply not about you. Yes it may *affect* you, but don't make it *about* you. Don't waste your time wondering why someone responded in the manner they did, didn't greet you the way you expected, or treated you unfairly. Move on. He may have rushed by you because his wife just called to pick up their sick child at school. It's not about you. She may have snapped at you because her boss just yelled at her. It's not about you. He might have overlooked you because he's preoccupied with his father's recent diagnosis. It's not about you. Don't waste your energy making it about you. Move on.

SIMPLE TRUTH

"Do not accuse anyone for no reason—when they have done you no harm."
Proverbs 3:30 (NIV)

SIMPLE TOOL

Don't take everything personally.

Recall a recent experience when you took something too personally. Now, take an honest look at the situation again and journal what actually happened. What did you tell yourself? What did you make that mean? What did it really mean?

27

WORDS OF WISDOM

KEEP YOUR WORDS FEW.

When asked a question, simply answer the question. There's no need to justify your response. If your answer isn't sufficient, you'll be asked another question. Too often, we fall into the trap of over-explaining, substantiating, or defending our positions. Just answer the question. Save the other person from listening to unnecessary details. Don't assume someone wants more information. If they need more or want more, they'll ask. There's no need to over-explain.

SIMPLE TRUTH

"Too much talk leads to sin. Be sensible and keep your mouth shut."
Proverbs 10:19 (NLT)

SIMPLE TOOL

Just answer the question.

For one day, keep a tally of all the times you accidentally say more than you mean to say (you know the feeling). Do you find yourself giving away bits of information you don't mean to? Note how often this occurs in your conversations.

Check a circle each time you say more than you mean to.

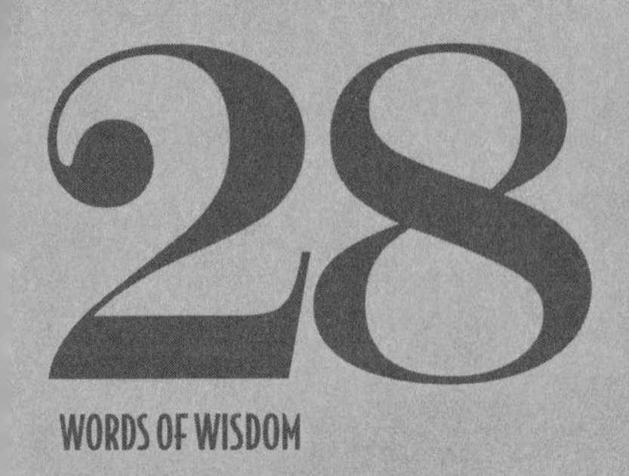

WORDS OF WISDOM

ALL STORMS END.

When you see the waves of turbulent times rolling towards you, stand still. Don't try to outrun what appears to be a tidal wave. Most often, the waves of pain won't be as destructive as you predict. The natural tendency is to try to dodge, hide, or escape from any form of discomfort or pain. Frequently, the storm will dissipate and the waves will only hit you knee-high. The energy you'll expend trying to anticipate the path of the storm or trying to outrun it often far exceeds what actually comes ashore. Conserve your energy and stand still. The waves of pain are inevitable, but they don't have to pull you under.

SIMPLE TRUTH

"Can all your worries add a single moment to your life?"
Matthew 6:27 (NLT)

SIMPLE TOOL

Acknowledge your fear.

Where are you experiencing fear or worry today? Stop running. Don't deny your fears. List each one—be descriptive.

Now list one small step you will take today to begin to conquer your fears.

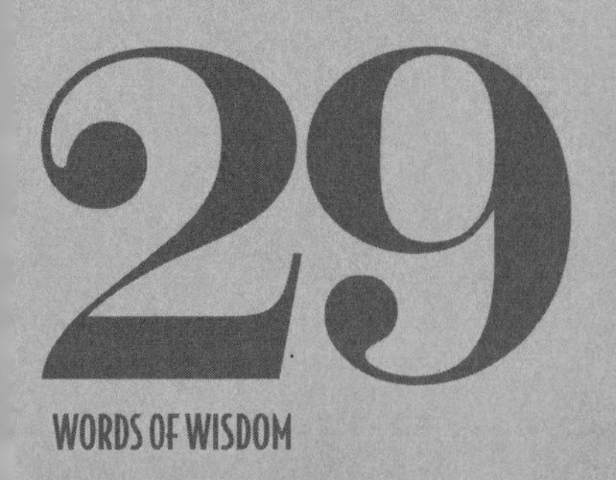

WORDS OF WISDOM

IF YOU DON'T TAKE THE FIRST STEP, YOU WON'T GO ANYWHERE.

If you wait until you have it all together first, you'll never do anything. What might you wait for? Yourself, your career, your plan, your finances, etc. It just isn't possible to prepare for every scenario. So prepare as best as you can, and expect a delay or detour now and again. That's okay. They were designed to alter your path, not to stop or discourage you. Remember, anyone who has dared to accomplish something great, dared to take the first step.

SIMPLE TRUTH

"This is my command—be strong and courageous! Do not be afraid or discouraged. For the LORD your God is with you wherever you go."
Joshua 1:9 (NLT)

SIMPLE TOOL

Step and move forward.

Taking the first step is the hardest. Review a current goal or plan. Write down one step you will take today that would move you closer to achieving it. If that step seems too big, break it down into even smaller steps. Put pen to paper. Then take the first step!

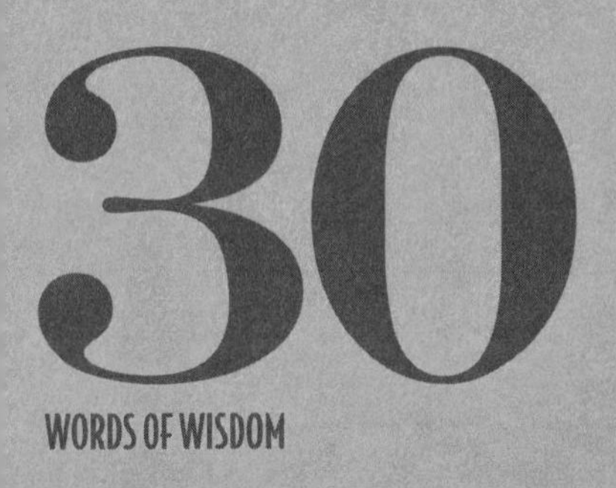

FIND ANSWERS IN THE RIGHT QUESTIONS.

Successful people have learned to get to the heart of the matter by asking better questions. Asking 'why?' can keep you running in circles. When you're looking for answers, ask yourself: *What's the message in this experience for me? What's the gift in this situation? What would I do if I took the fear factor away? What small step can I take today? What's the most loving thing I can say or do now? What would I do if I knew I couldn't fail? What can I learn from this?* These questions will propel you forward. Drop the 'why?' and ask 'what?'

SIMPLE TRUTH

"Trust in the LORD with all your heart and lean not on your own understanding."
Proverbs 3:5 (NIV)

SIMPLE TOOL

Sometimes only God knows 'why.' Ask, 'what?'

What questions do you have? List each question.
Begin each with 'What...'

This will get you started:

What ____?

What ____?

What ____?

What ____?

What ____?

What ____?

What ____?

FORGIVENESS RELEASES YOU.

Forgiveness is the key that releases you. Forgive those who've abused, hurt, or offended you. Remember that wounded people wound people. Forgiving others releases you from the burden of carrying the anger and pain that would otherwise hold you captive. If you want to be free, forgive. Choosing to forgive unlocks the door to freedom.

SIMPLE TRUTH

"Be kind and compassionate to one another, forgiving each other, just as in Christ God forgave you."
Ephesians 4:32 (NIV)

SIMPLE TOOL

Choose to forgive.

List all the people you need to forgive. Be specific about the offense for which you need to forgive them. Here's the big challenge: List some of the many ways God has forgiven you. This will help you forgive others.

Person	Offense

Ways God has forgiven me:

1

2

3

32
WORDS OF WISDOM

BE WHO YOU ARE.

When you accept the fact that not everyone will like you, your style, your mannerisms, or the way you communicate, you free yourself to be yourself. The sooner you learn this simple truth, the sooner you'll free yourself to live in the magnificence of who God created you to be. Let's face it, not everyone has the same taste in art, music, or food, so don't expect everyone to appreciate your uniqueness.

SIMPLE TRUTH

"For you created my inmost being; you knit me together in my mother's womb."
Psalm 139:13 (NIV)

SIMPLE TOOL

Embrace your uniqueness.

How do you see yourself? List all the wonderful ways God made you. How will you celebrate your uniqueness? Consider writing God a thank you note to appreciate how He created you.

WORDS OF WISDOM

WHEN YOU'RE A PRIORITY, YOU'LL KNOW.

When someone wants to be with you, they will. People make time for what's most important to them. When you're a priority, you'll know. Watch. Listen. Learn. When you're a priority in someone's life, you'll see, hear from, and be with them. It's just that simple. Don't make excuses for someone's lack of interest in you. In other words, when someone wants to be with you, they'll rearrange their schedule to make it happen. They won't just throw you a leftover crumb. God never intended you to feast on the crumbs; He wants you to have the whole pie.

SIMPLE TRUTH

"For where your treasure is, there your heart will be also."
Luke 12:34 (NIV)

SIMPLE TOOL

Pay attention to your relationships.

List the significant relationships in your life. Indicate next to each person the percentage of time you sense they invest in the relationship. Then, ask yourself how much time *you're* investing in *them*. (For example: John invests 30%; I invest 90%.) The numbers speak for themselves.

Name	Their %	My %

WORDS OF WISDOM

YOU STAND STRONGEST ON YOUR KNEES.

Is God your Commanding Officer? If so, drop and give Him five! Hit the deck first thing every morning. Drop to your knees and give Him your first five minutes alone. Give God your mind, mouth, and movements. This exercise will strengthen your spirit and body. It will allow you to start your day with God and move forward in His power with confidence.

SIMPLE TRUTH

"Three times a day he got down on his knees and prayed, giving thanks to his God, just as he had done before."
Daniel 6:10 (NIV)

SIMPLE TOOL

Make time to pray.

How much time do you dedicate to prayer daily?

What hinders your prayer life?

Write down three specific prayer requests. If you're not praying, how do you expect God to answer?

1

2

3

DAY 34

WORDS OF WISDOM

THERE'S A FINE LINE BETWEEN DEDICATION AND FOOLISHNESS.

Being dedicated to someone or something means you're committed, devoted, and faithful. How do you know when you've crossed the line into the land of foolishness? When your dedication turns to compulsion, fixation, or preoccupation, you've crossed it. Be dedicated to your family, career, and cause. And be mindful. Don't turn a good thing into an unhealthy addiction, idol, or obsession.

SIMPLE TRUTH

"You must not have any other god but me."
Exodus 20:3 (NLT)

SIMPLE TOOL

Be dedicated, not foolish.

Who or what are you putting before your relationship with God? Do you spend more time watching TV, at work, or hanging out with your friends than with God? Write down five concrete actions you'll take this week to put God first. Consider waking up earlier, shutting off all devices, or taking a prayer walk.

1

2

3

4

5

TAKE PEOPLE AT THEIR WORD.

It doesn't take long to understand someone's true character and intentions. Listen carefully. Don't edit or rewrite what they said. And for heaven's sake, don't revise their words to fit your desire or wishful fantasy. Take them at their word.

SIMPLE TRUTH

"But their evil intentions will be exposed when the light shines on them."
Ephesians 5:13 (NLT)

SIMPLE TOOL

People tell you who they are. Believe them.

If you're experiencing pain, betrayal, or disappointment in a relationship, go back to when you first met; write down everything you remember about your early conversations. Often, you'll discover you chose to overlook what was actually said.

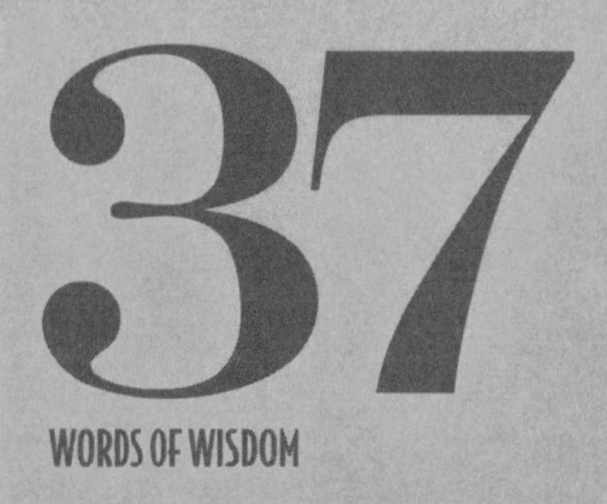

WORDS OF WISDOM

NO ONE IS A MIND READER.

A surefire way to get frustrated is to expect someone to know what you want without telling them. If you want someone to respond in a particular way or do something in a specific manner, simply tell them. Don't expect anyone to read your mind. Simply say what you mean.

SIMPLE TRUTH

"Then his disciples said, 'At last you are speaking plainly and not figuratively.'"
John 16:29 (NLT)

SIMPLE TOOL

Communicate your needs clearly.

Be clear in your own mind first. Write down what you need. Then, calmly, slowly, and concisely share your needs. Afterwards, simply ask the other person if they have any questions. Don't assume they understood you.

My Needs:

1 ______________________________

2 ______________________________

3 ______________________________

4 ______________________________

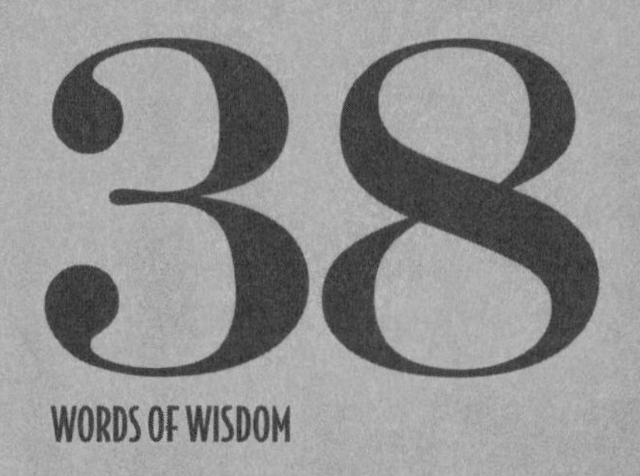

WORDS OF WISDOM

EVERY DAY IS REASON TO CELEBRATE!

Don't wait for your birthday, a special holiday, or a promotion to celebrate. Create an opportunity today and celebrate. Why? Because you're alive and you can! Turn a typical Tuesday into a celebration. Burn those expensive candles. Go ahead, put on your favorite dress! Who cares that you're only going to run errands? You don't have to wait for an invitation to celebrate. Today's the gift, so open it and celebrate!

SIMPLE TRUTH

"This is the day the LORD has made. We will rejoice and be glad in it."
Psalm 118:24 (NLT)

SIMPLE TOOL

Celebrate this day.

List five creative ways you will celebrate this day. It doesn't have to cost much. The point is to have some fun. This day won't come again.

1 ______________________

2 ______________________

3 ______________________

4 ______________________

5 ______________________

You don't have to use all of your ideas today. Save some to celebrate tomorrow!

WORDS OF WISDOM

YOU TEACH PEOPLE HOW TO TREAT YOU.

You're always teaching people how to treat you. You teach them by what you say *and* by what you don't say. When you put up with intolerable behavior because you're either too afraid or too uncomfortable to say something, you're silently giving someone permission to treat you that way. When you don't speak up and set healthy boundaries, you're teaching others to trample over you. You're responsible for setting your boundaries and teaching others how to treat you. Speak up!

SIMPLE TRUTH

"Guard your heart above all else, for it determines the course of your life."
Proverbs 4:23 (NLT)

SIMPLE TOOL

Don't let people walk on you. You're not a doormat.

Where do you need to set boundaries? Before confronting someone, be sure you're clear how you've allowed these boundaries to be crossed in the past. Start your conversation by acknowledging your role and by clearly stating your preferences going forward. Write your thoughts out here first.

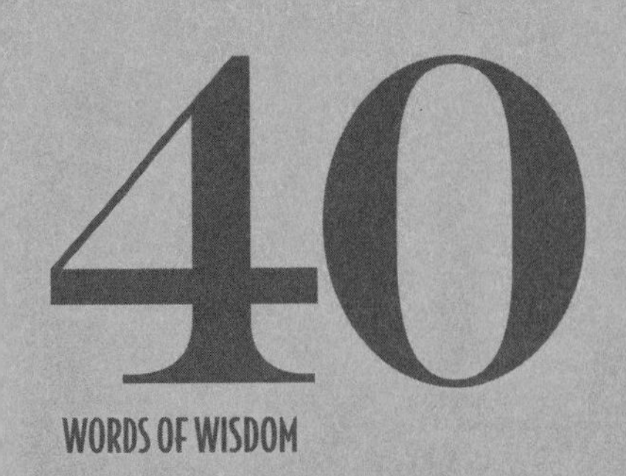

WORDS OF WISDOM

IF YOU BOTTLE YOUR FEELINGS, EVENTUALLY THEY'LL POP OUT.

How long do you think you can hold a beach ball under water? *Answer:* You don't know. In which direction will the beach ball go when it surfaces? *Answer:* Again, you don't know. The same is true regarding your feelings. When you try to contain them by holding them down, you never know when, where, or how they'll pop out. What's the point? Learn to communicate your feelings in a healthy manner and at an appropriate time. When you stuff your feelings, you can be sure they'll surface when you least expect it, and they'll likely hit an unintended victim.

SIMPLE TRUTH

"There is nothing concealed that will not be disclosed, or hidden that will not be made known."
Luke 12:2 (NIV)

SIMPLE TOOL

Release your tension.

There is physical activity involved with letting go of negativity. Try these ideas or come up with your own. They might sound ridiculous, but you will feel better afterward.

1 Sit in your car and scream at the top of your lungs with the windows closed. Just scream.

2 Go for a run or take a kickboxing class.

3 Go to the beach and kick sand or pound the water.

4 Rip up an old phonebook.

Which idea will you start with?

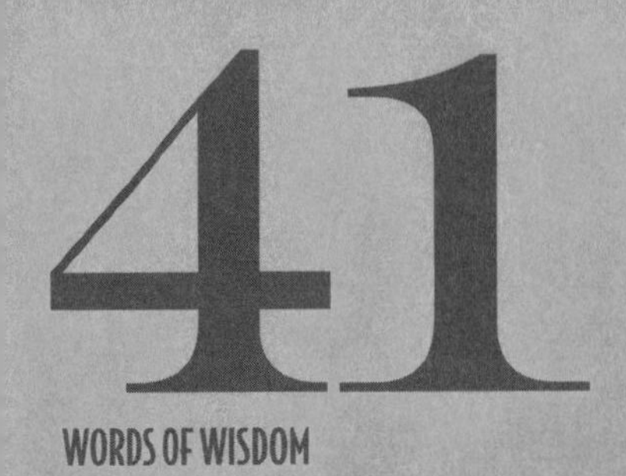

WORDS OF WISDOM

WE GIVE PEOPLE WHAT *WE* WANT, NOT WHAT *THEY* NEED.

When you see someone in pain or in need, ask, "What does support look like from me, to you, at this time?" You'll be surprised what you learn. Frequently you'll hear, "I don't know. No one has ever asked me that before." This straightforward question is powerful for two reasons. First, it takes the responsibility off you to figure out what someone needs and places it on the person in need. It empowers them to tell you what they need, while removing the guesswork for you. Second, it helps you respond to their needs as you are able. One of two things will happen: You'll be able to meet their need, or you won't. In either case, ask the question and give what you can.

SIMPLE TRUTH

"Do nothing out of selfish ambition or vain conceit. Rather, in humility value others above yourselves."
Philippians 2:3 (NIV)

SIMPLE TOOL

Ask, "What does support look like from me, to you, at this time?"

The next time you see someone in need, simply ask, "What does support look like from me, to you, at this time?" Then just listen, and give what you can.

Who do you know who needs support right now? Go ask them this question. What did they say?

What does support look like for you?

Remember to share your answer the next time you need support.

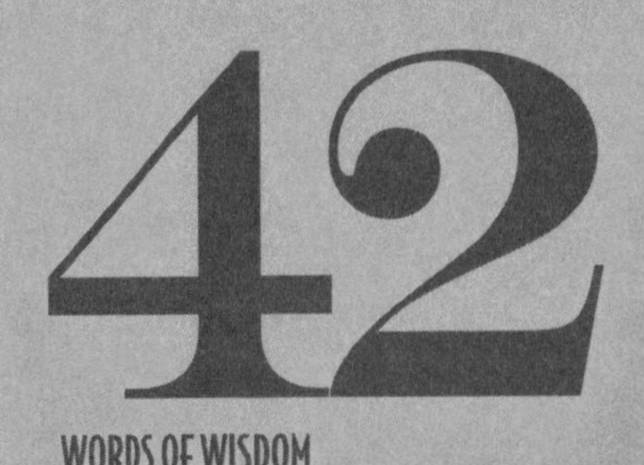

WORDS OF WISDOM

SERVE WHERE YOUR FEET ARE PLANTED.

There are countless opportunities to help and serve every day. Start your day by simply asking, "God, who needs my help today? Open my eyes to see that person and to hear their quiet cry for help." Then as you move through your day, be open to seeing and responding to those opportunities. Sometimes, the occasion will present itself at the grocery store when you meet a harried cashier who needs encouragement. Other times, your phone will ring and you'll simply be asked to listen to a friend in need. The call to serve doesn't require traveling to a foreign country. Your mission field is where your feet are planted today—here and now. Be the difference.
Just do something!

SIMPLE TRUTH

"God has given each of you a gift from his great variety of spiritual gifts. Use them well to serve one another."
1 Peter 4:10 (NLT)

SIMPLE TOOL

Do something. Someone needs your help today.

You don't have to wait for someone to ask for help. Write down three people who are in need. After each name, identify one small way you will be of service. Make a meal for a new mom, offer to bring a neighbor's child home from school, or pick up some groceries for a friend. List your ideas.

Person in Need

1 ____________________

2 ____________________

3 ____________________

1 Way to Serve

1 ____________________

2 ____________________

3 ____________________

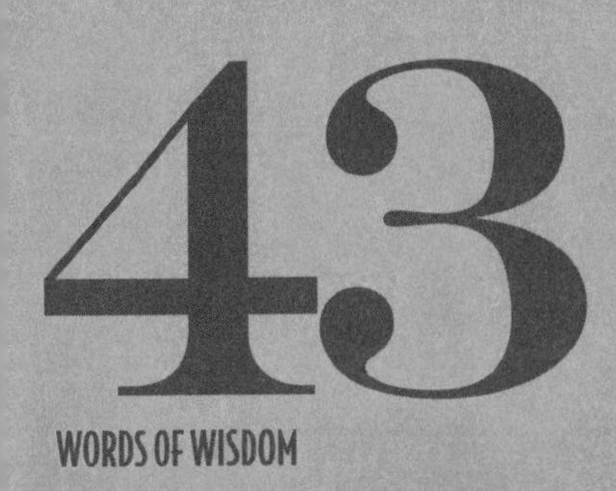

WORDS OF WISDOM

SHINE YOUR LIGHT.

Have you ever known a person who, after they walk away, you think to yourself, *I want to be more like them?* Chances are, they have the symptoms of a positively contagious spirit: optimistic, encouraging, inspiring, genuine, passionate, and enthusiastic. Conversely, a person with a highly contaminated spirit bears very different symptoms: pessimistic, controlling, grumbling, and argumentative. Is your spirit positively contagious or highly contaminated? Do people walk away from you infected with your toxic negativity, or are you filling them with joy and light?

SIMPLE TRUTH

"Let your light shine before others."
Matthew 5:16 (NIV)

SIMPLE TOOL

Shine brightly.

Dare to ask three trusted friends, family members, or coworkers this question: "How do you see me?" Ask them to write their thoughts down on paper. Review their responses. What similarities are there? What surprised you? How can you be a more positive person?

Similarities:

Surprises:

Steps to be a more positive person:

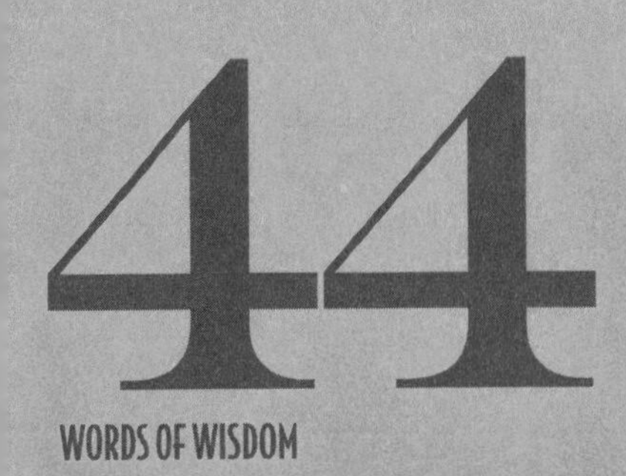

WORDS OF WISDOM

YOU CHOOSE WHERE TO INVEST YOUR ENERGY.

You determine when and how you'll expend your energy. Envision a jar with a lid. Imagine inside that jar is your allotted energy for each day. It's your responsibility to determine for whom and for how long you'll use that energy. Each time you remove the lid, you're giving a little more of your energy away. Remember, your energy should be preserved and distributed carefully. Before opening the jar and dispensing your limited energy, ask yourself, "Can I afford to invest in this cause, conversation, or person at this moment? Do I have enough energy left?" Remember, no one can steal your energy—you give it away. Open your jar cautiously and use your energy wisely.

SIMPLE TRUTH

"Don't waste what is holy on people who are unholy."
Matthew 7:6 (NLT)

SIMPLE TOOL

Use your energy wisely.

For three days, carry a notebook and jot down how you spend each hour. Keep it brief. Then, review your notes and list the areas where you are depleting your energy. The best way to preserve your energy is to know where you're using it.

Things That Drain My Energy:

BE HOSPITABLE.

Life is unpredictable. Therefore, always reserve an open seat for the unexpected guest. Set the table of your life with the anticipation that God will bring someone for you to serve at any moment. When you intentionally open your home and save a place for an impromptu visitor, you'll always be prepared to nourish them with hope, love, and the spiritual food to sustain them on their journey.

SIMPLE TRUTH

"Do not forget to show hospitality to strangers, for by so doing some people have shown hospitality to angels without knowing it."
Hebrews 13:2 (NIV)

SIMPLE TOOL

Open your heart and home.

Showing hospitality is more than inviting someone to dinner. Come up with some creative ways you will practice hospitality. Or, try one of these: invite a neighbor for a walk, offer to watch a friend's child while she runs some errands, or mail homemade treats to a college student.

List creative ways to practice hospitality:

Write down one way you will practice hospitality this week:

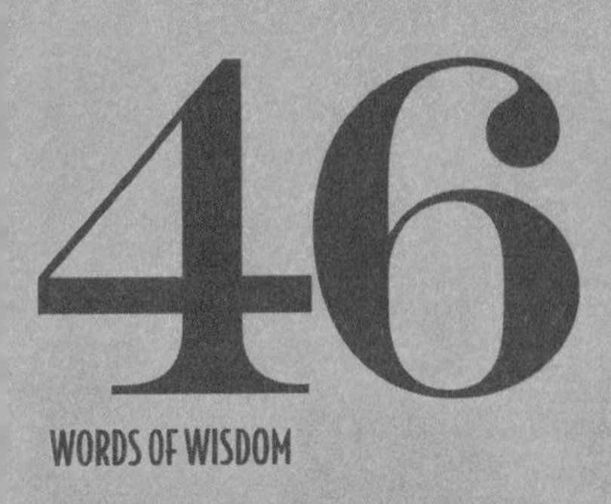

WORDS OF WISDOM

OPERATING ON AUTOPILOT ISN'T LIVING; IT'S EXISTING.

Most people move through their days on autopilot. Each morning, commit to experience your day with a different mindset—eyes wide open, highly in tune with God and your surroundings. When you make the conscious decision to take yourself off autopilot, you make yourself available to see and receive the boundless miracles around you. You'll know the events in your life don't just happen randomly. Rather, they unfold according to God's timing and under His direction and authority. You'll experience the synergy of events that will conspire to help you live every moment on purpose and with purpose.

SIMPLE TRUTH

"Wake up, sleeper."
Ephesians 5:14 (NIV)

SIMPLE TOOL

Be mindful.

You can be mindful about a number of activities that you typically do without much thought, such as: eating, washing dishes, cooking, taking a bath or shower, walking, driving in the car, or listening to music. Do one activity at a time and then journal your thoughts. This takes daily practice.

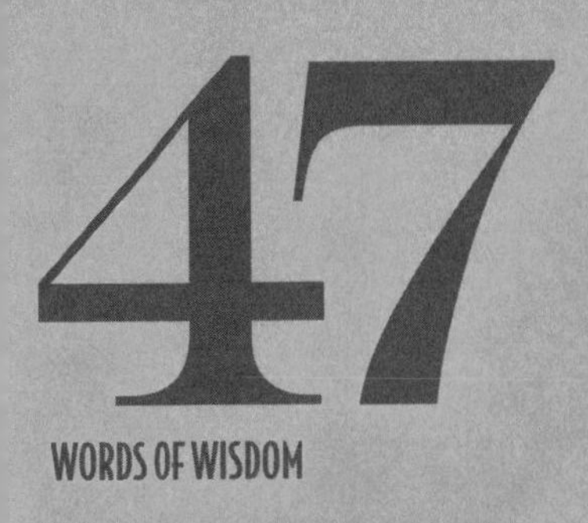

WORDS OF WISDOM

YOU CAN'T HEAR GOD AMIDST ALL THE NOISE AND CHATTER.

One of the most lucrative investments you'll ever make is to Take 10 daily. There are 1,440 minutes in each day. Intentionally carve out 10 of those 1,440 minutes to simply be. Choose to be still and listen. Taking 10 affords you the opportunity to be quiet with your thoughts. Until you're silent and alone, it's hard to discern God's still small voice. Take 10 daily; you'll be glad you did.

SIMPLE TRUTH

"Be still, and know that I am God."
Psalm 46:10 (NIV)

SIMPLE TOOL

Be still.

Being still is nothing more than intentional rest. Commit to being still for ten minutes each day. Then, simply write down what came up in those ten minutes. There is no right answer. Just pay attention.

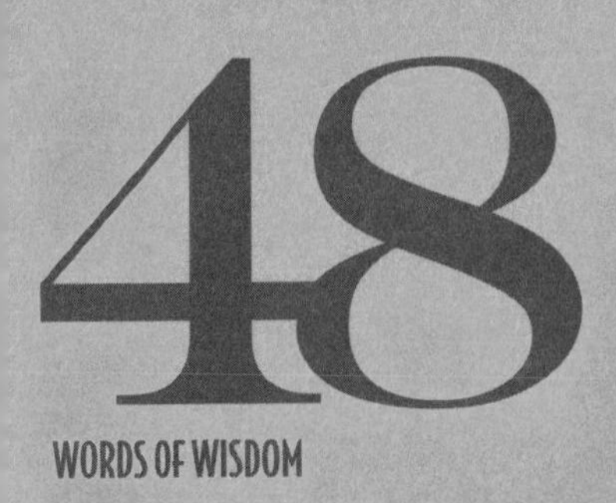

WORDS OF WISDOM

JOY IS EVERYWHERE. GRAB IT.

Joy is what makes life beautiful. It's what can get you through the difficult times. Joy is what brings levity to your heart. Joy heals your heartache, inspires you to greatness, and fills you with goodness. Live this day with joy and expectancy, like the child who eagerly digs through a box of Cracker Jacks® in search of the hidden toy. Grasp and embrace the simple surprises. Let them bring joy to your day!

SIMPLE TRUTH

"A joyful heart is good medicine."
Proverbs 17:22 (ESV)

SIMPLE TOOL

Find joy in simple surprises.

Make a list of the simple things that bring you joy. Then, capture joy by incorporating those simple things into your day. Remember that increasing your joy doesn't have to be expensive.

1

2

3

4

5

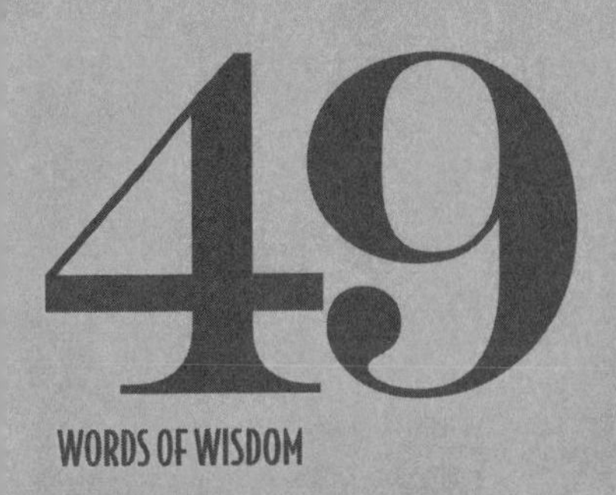

WORDS OF WISDOM

LOOK TO JESUS.

You will become like that which you focus your attention upon. Therefore, turn your eyes toward Jesus and away from your circumstances. When you look to anyone or anything other than Jesus, you will become distracted and lose sight of Him. Remember, Peter could walk on water when he fixed his eyes on Jesus. It was only after Peter looked away and was frightened by the waves that he began to sink. Look up!

SIMPLE TRUTH

"We do this by keeping our eyes on Jesus."
Hebrews 12:2 (NLT)

SIMPLE TOOL

Fix your eyes on Jesus.

What are you focusing on right now? If you don't fix your attention on God and His power and strength, then you'll feel anxious, confused, or overwhelmed! Harness your thoughts and focus on God.

COLLECT PEARLS OF WISDOM.

You can never gain enough wisdom. When you are wise, you will listen and add to your collection of pearls. You will eagerly approach every conversation anticipating and hunting for the pearl. You will look beyond your preconceived notions and search for it in every opportunity. You will leave your inner critic behind, the one who sizes people up based on appearances and delivery style, and yearn to learn something of value from all. Wisdom comes to those who seek it. Wisdom comes to those who ask. Turn your ear to wisdom. When you do, you will walk away with a priceless strand of precious pearls to pass down to future generations.

SIMPLE TRUTH

"If you prize wisdom, she will make you great. Embrace her, and she will honor you. She will place a lovely wreath on your head; she will present you with a beautiful crown."
Proverbs 4:8-9 (NLT)

SIMPLE TOOL

Hunt for pearls of wisdom.

Commit to listening for the pearl of wisdom. Go into every conversation today determined to leave with a jewel. Record what you learned.

What did you notice about yourself? Your listening habits?

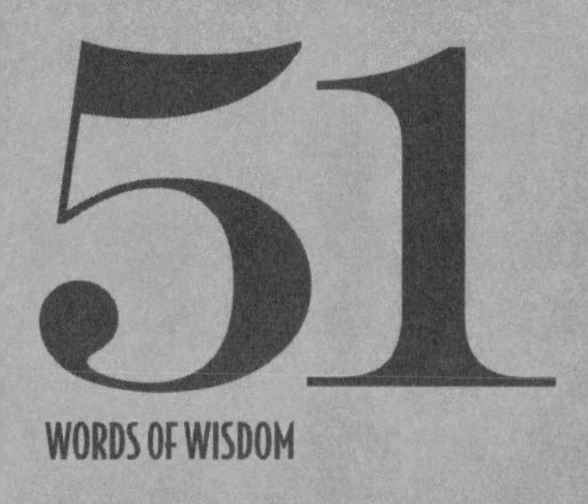

WORDS OF WISDOM

YOU CAN'T STUFF GOD IN A BOX.

You might conveniently store your personal gods in a small comfortable box, but God is too big to fit in your God-in-the-box thinking. If you're trying to get God to fit into your plans and desires, you'll always be frustrated. Reverse roles and ask, "How can I fit into God's plan?" Then you'll discover the peace you have been searching for. Remember God is bigger than your theology, your understanding, and you. If you close the box on God, chances are you've closed your heart on Him too. You cannot walk with God and be the god of your life at the same time. You must choose. Choose wisely.

SIMPLE TRUTH

"(God) is able to do immeasurably more than all we ask or imagine, according to his power that is at work within us."
Ephesians 3:20 (NIV)

SIMPLE TOOL

Take God out of the box.

List all the ways you have been limiting God.
Where have you shut the lid on His plans and timing?

What small step will you take today to be more open to His will?

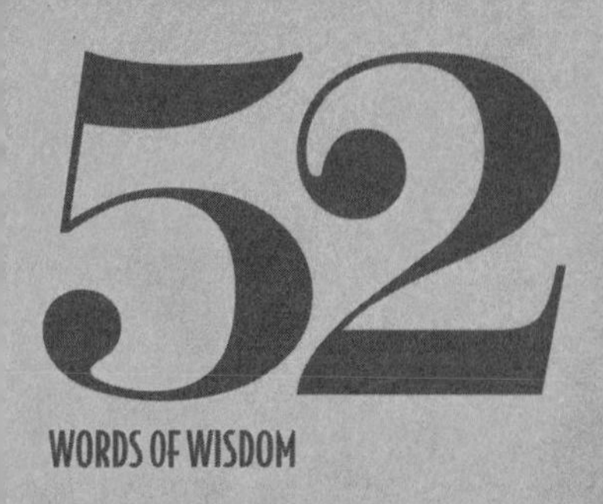

WORDS OF WISDOM

GOD IS NOT FINISHED YET.

Wherever you are in your faith right now, God says that you are not yet where you will be. How exciting is that? You're right where you are for a reason. You're exactly where God wants you. When He's ready to move you, He will. Rest in knowing God is in control. He's got you. He's putting His fingerprints all over your life. Though you may not feel His presence, know He's in every detail. Be okay with not knowing the end of the story. When you know God is the Author and Finisher of your life, you can trust you're in good hands. You're in His hands. "Everything's DAPO!" It's in God's Divine And Perfect Order. Trust that God is not finished with you yet!

SIMPLE TRUTH

"You do not realize now what I am doing, but later you will understand."
John 13:7 (NIV)

SIMPLE TOOL

Trust God with the details.

How would your perspective change today if you believed that in time you will understand what God is doing, even if you don't right now? Journal your dreams, expectations, and desires for your future and trust God with the details.

MEET ME

I put off writing this part of the book until I was told in no uncertain terms, *"We need your bio today, Susan!"*

After countless revisions, and equally as many trips to the kitchen refrigerator, as if I could somehow magically find my words behind the Tupperware bowl, I decided there was only one way I knew how to answer difficult questions like, *"Who are you?"* and *"What do you hope your readers will get from your book?"* The answer lies in this simple true story:

During a job interview in 1998, I faced a question that forever changed the trajectory of my life. The VP of Sales asked, *"What's the most important position you've ever held? And, what did you learn in that role?"* The moment of truth came in that brief silent pause before I answered. I knew I had a choice: I could give a politically correct corporate answer, or I could speak my truth. I chose the latter.

I confidently responded, "I was a waitress at the country club in high school." Upon seeing her less-than-impressed look with my answer, I proceeded to share what those hungry customers taught me, and what I believe most people still hunger for today. People yearn to be:

1. Seen
2. Heard
3. And, understood.

Yes, I got that job. I stayed four years. Then in 2002, I left to follow my calling, to help people know they are seen, heard, and understood. I opened my personal and professional coaching practice. After ten years of coaching, my clients encouraged me to write this book and share my life lessons. Now, I travel the country speaking at corporate events and women's conferences. I love it!

I am hungry to tell you that I see you, I hear you, and although I may not know *your* pain, I do understand pain. And, you are not alone.

Please join me in the private Facebook group I've created just for you to share what you're learning and going through. You'll find other readers there, too. We *all* want to feel like we belong.

www.facebook.com/groups/DivineAndPerfectOrder

If you'd like to have me speak at your event, I'd love to chat.
Just call me at 224.484.0564.

THANK YOU

I have an incredible cast of DAPO supporters. Thank you for walking with me on this journey.

My wonderful husband Greg, you keep me laughing while insisting I'm the source for all of your material. Thank you for enthusiastically supporting all of my crazy ideas. I love you, Bucket!

Steve Hoeft of Raising The Standard, LLC, you indeed raise the standard on everything you touch. You assembled an outstanding team.

Cat Knarr, your attention to detail, dedication to your craft, and spirit of excellence are a rare find. I treasure you, editor extraordinaire.

Gaige Larson, you breathed life into this book with your creative and vibrant design.

Dee DeFrates, aka GFD, your friendship, prayers, and amazing sense of humor keep me going. Thank you for always reminding me to be true to my voice, and for being my *truth* friend.

Gina Lindberg and Sarah Marentette, your faithful prayers and constant support sustain me.

Liz Molli, thank you for believing in DAPO from the beginning and for crossing the Finish Line with me.

THOUGHTS & ACTION STEPS

THOUGHTS & ACTION STEPS

THOUGHTS & ACTION STEPS

THOUGHTS & ACTION STEPS

THOUGHTS & ACTION STEPS

THOUGHTS & ACTION STEPS

THOUGHTS & ACTION STEPS

THOUGHTS & ACTION STEPS